MINIMIZING TRANSITION LOSS

MINIMIZING TRANSITION LOSS

The Hand-off from Middle School to High School

Carol J. Christian, C. Thomas Potter II, and Kevin S. Koett

ROWMAN & LITTLEFIELD
Lanham • Boulder • New York • London

Published by Rowman & Littlefield
An imprint of The Rowman & Littlefield Publishing Group, Inc.
4501 Forbes Boulevard, Suite 200, Lanham, Maryland 20706
www.rowman.com

Unit A, Whitacre Mews, 26-34 Stannary Street, London SE11 4AB

Copyright © 2018 by Carol J. Christian, C. Thomas Potter II, and Kevin S. Koett

All rights reserved. No part of this book may be reproduced in any form or by any electronic or mechanical means, including information storage and retrieval systems, without written permission from the publisher, except by a reviewer who may quote passages in a review.

British Library Cataloguing in Publication Information Available

Library of Congress Cataloging-in-Publication Data Available

ISBN 978-1-4758-4270-8 (cloth : alk. paper)
ISBN 978-1-4758-4271-5 (pbk. : alk. paper)
ISBN 978-1-4758-4272-2 (electronic)

∞ ™ The paper used in this publication meets the minimum requirements of American National Standard for Information Sciences Permanence of Paper for Printed Library Materials, ANSI/NISO Z39.48-1992.

Printed in the United States of America

CONTENTS

Preface vii
Introduction xi

1 Fear of Swirlies 1
2 They Called Him Stinky 7
3 Locker Room Horror Stories 13
4 Cut—Disconnected—Drifting 19
5 Parents in the Transition 25
6 Dad's in Jail, Mom's Always High, and I Live with my Grandparents 31
7 Above His Raisin' 35
8 Home Visits 41
9 Dual Credit, Apprenticeships, Career Academies 47
10 Does Anybody Hear Me? Does Anybody See Me? Does Anybody Care? 51
11 "Withit" High School 57
12 Questions . . . Questions . . . Questions 65

About the Authors 71

PREFACE

Transitions are a part of life. Everyone must go through them to get to the next level. Whether transitioning from grade to grade, leaving an old familiar building for a newer one or moving to a new place as a parent relocates the entire family, everyone, both students and parents, will go through a period of adjustment during the transition.

Moving from middle school to high school can be one of the most critical transitions students will make in their educational career. Historically, grade nine is known as the freshman bulge. In many schools across the country, grade nine has the highest student enrollment due in part to the number of students repeating grade nine.

While students are in middle school and about to enter high school, these "tweeners"—those students caught in the middle between adolescence and adulthood—many times struggle to find their niche on their way to developing into more fully actualized human beings.

Brand name clothes that were never important before become the center of argument when parents cannot afford what the student wants. Those once soft-skinned angelic baby faces are suddenly replaced by braces, zits, and eyeglasses brought on by a myriad number of hormonal changes. Kids that loved school up until this point begin to lose focus as they put at the core of their existence the superficial things of fitting in or being popular as these things become more important than academic performance. It is here where this age student can become lost in the transition.

This book will likely conjure up a number of scenarios that the reader can relate to from their transition from middle school to high school. The important thing to realize is that educators, schools, and institutions can do something about it to improve it for the next generation of learners!

We do not have to send our students forth in blind ignorance of what is just beyond the classroom walls at the next level. It is the little things, the transition activities that educators can intentionally design and implement, that can make a world of difference in creating a smooth transition for the student and therefore lessen the likelihood of a student becoming a drop-out statistic by grade ten.

Numerous theorists have studied human growth and development. This book examines the work of researchers Maslow, Levinson, Vygotsky, Erikson, and Keniston, and attempts to connect theory with practice. The transition activities attempt to put the theory to practice. These activities are researched based, more common sense than theory, and easier to implement than most schools care to admit.

Many middle and high schools believe that implementing such activities is a waste of time and energy. They operate under the belief that this age student needs to grow up and realize they are no longer in elementary school. But the author of this book, Carol J. Christian, a highly recognized and successful educator and administrator, operates under the premise that, "we are all little people in big people's bodies."

We are all on a path of learning toward self-growth, self-acceptance, and self-discovery. Similarly, adults have fears about the new job, the same job but being transferred to a different location, to the promotion that causes us, with life experiences, much inner turmoil and trepidation. As adults we too appreciate the mentoring programs, the first-year employee seminars, the orientation periods that transitioned us toward success. Let us work collaboratively to create a smooth transition for these young people under our charge during the transition from middle school to high school.

INTRODUCTION

This book focuses primarily on the middle to high school transition. *Minimizing Transition Loss: The Hand-off from Middle School to High School* is one in a series of three separate but inter-related books that share scenarios of what it is like on the journey through schooling and the obstacles students often face during each transition.

Educators and parents need to make a concerted effort to better understand the developmental differences of middle school and early grade level high school students. This age learner often vacillates back and forth between acting like an adolescent and acting like a young adult. Teachers and parents can either blindly send these students on to high school in the hope that they can make the needed adjustments to be successful, or we can intentionally implement transition activities that are researched based with the goal of improving their chances of a smooth transition.

There is no question that the middle school and high school years are some of the more difficut, tumultuous, and complex grade levels of learning students will navigate while they deal with many physical and emotional changes during this developmental stage of their life. There is help and hope for these students if they are fortunate enough to be a student in a school that truly understands that students may grow in height at a rapid rate, but their inner growth, their emotional and mental growth, have not yet caught up. Educators must help students during this physical transformation and transition to another school, another grade.

This work is developed with a two-fold premise: one, that educators and parents understand the role they play in meeting the basic developomental needs of individual students during times of transition; and two, that school leaders understand how critically important it is for organizations to create structured transition processes to better ensure student success before, during, and after transitions that support the growth and development of students.

Transition success does not happen by chance. Schools must intentionally develop activities that make it easier for students to have an effective transition experience. As students navigate each move through the K-12 and postsecondary school systems, multiple transitions occur that include but are not limited to moving to different and unfamiliar school buildings, and going from self-contained classrooms with one teacher to departmentalized schools with numerous teachers. Most building transitions require a move to larger, more impersonal school environments. It is during these periods of transition that students can become lost in the shuffle as they move through multiple period days, various teacher routines and expectations, more complex schedules, increased academic rigor, and growth and developmental changes. Each of these transitions can pose barriers to ensuring student success.

Many students who lack the support structures from school and home that can help ensure a seamless transition become lost in transition. These students many times begin to experience an increase in failing grades and an increase in inappropriate behaviors. As a result of frustration, fear, and the inability to cope with the stresses, many students increase their risk of becoming a drop-out statistic.

The research that served as the foundational structure for this book centered on transition research and Maslow's understanding of human growth and development. The literature support serves to assist educators and parents in understanding why it is important to intervene with a purposeful set of transition plans and activities that are intentionally developed to help students during each move from grade to grade, school to school, or high school to postsecondary.

This book is both practitioner based and parent friendly. The book is written in authentic scenarios combined with research-based suggested intervention strategies to help combat the barriers associated with the transitional moves middle school students may experience. It is a goal of this work and its companion books that school organizations and institutions will work collectively to strategically develop district-wide and inter-agency (high school and college) transition plans to help students during these critical periods.

In understanding human growth and basic levels of human need, educators come to better understand the total child: physically, socially, emotionally, and intellectually. In this era of high-stakes accountability, educators must not lose sight of reaching out to students at a deeper, more basic level than merely teaching content. Educators and parents would serve students well in being reminded of the inner, human developmental needs of our students and what schools can intentionally do to ensure successful transitions by implementing transition activies that prepare them for these moves.

Educators often study in college the theory of learning. It is a goal of these authors that in using real life stories, the connections can be made in bridging theory with practice while providing suggestions for interventions that can be strategically embedded in individualized transition plans.

I

FEAR OF SWIRLIES

Parents many times laugh at child's fear of being cornered in the bathroom in the transition from middle school to high school and the imagined terror of having their head stuck in a flushing toilet. Parents tell their child these are just stories, get tough, suck it up, and go on. But sadly, these nightmares can be real. These fears can cause some students to develop school sickness that begins the downward spiral of high absenteeism that ultimately impacts grades, academic promotion, and graduation.

Harassment and bullying has many faces. Educators and parents should not treat these fears lightly in their quest to create a successful transition from middle school to high school. We all have personal stories of something that transpired during our transition to high school. Stories that after all of these years still haunt us, stories we still cannot forget no matter how much we wish we could. Many have left scars that last a lifetime. Here is one child's story . . . what is yours?

VIGNETTE

Jonathan was always a strong student. He liked going to school. He liked reading. He dreamed of someday becoming a bio-genetic scientist. Jonathan was small in stature. He never really fit in with the cool kids as he was never much of an athlete. He was somewhat of an introvert and viewed by many of his classmates as a loner.

Like most eighth graders, Jonathan both dreaded and looked forward to the move from middle school to high school. His middle school was half the size of the high school he was transitioning to. His fears were many. He was anxious about getting lost and about not getting to class on time. He worried about the increased academic rigor and not being able to keep up with the high school workload. He worried about finding his niche, of making friends, and fitting in. Most of all, he worried about harassment from upperclassmen.

He had heard the stories of ninth graders being taken into the bathroom only to have their head flushed in a toilet. This ritual, he heard, was the initiation or rite of passage to senior high. The thought of that possibly happening brought him just short of a panic attack. He shared his inner feelings and concerns with his parents but they reassured him that those things just do not happen.

The second week of school Jonathan entered the bathroom during class change. He entered alone and found himself the only one using the facility. Preparing to leave was a different story. Three upperclassmen had entered the lavatory. In an instant Jonathan found himself being held upside down facing the porcelain pony. The fear, the humiliation, the horror were far greater than he had ever imagined. Life for Jonathan changed that day . . . forever. Jonathan never told his parents what happened. But word spread quickly within the school about the incident. Everywhere he went, classmates snickered. The story became bigger than life.

Soon, Jonathan began to find reasons for not going to school. Excuses started out as not feeling well. When he used up all of those, he began skipping school. His grades plummeted, his absences soared, and his dreams, one by one, began to fade. Jonathan turned sixteen his sophomore year in high school. One month later, he dropped out.

At the first class reunion, five years after his class graduated from high school, Jonathan's name still came up as people rehashed funny stories of those glory days in high school. Jonathan, however, never graduated from high school. The last people heard of him, he was driving a transit bus for the city living in a low-income housing project. He lived his adult life as he did his few short years in high school—alone.

If the truth be known, Jonathan's IQ was in the genius range. Think of what Jonathan could have been. Reflect on the contributions to society this gifted student could have left. Perhaps one of the clever youth that held him over the toilet that day lost a loved one to some dreaded disease—if Jonathan was left to fulfill his dream and develop his gifts, he could have cracked the code to cancer. Perhaps that loved one would be alive today.

Educators and parents should not gloss over student fears like those shared by the Jonathan's of the world. Educators and parents need to intentionally plan transition activities and work to ensure a safe transition to the new, often larger, more impersonal high school environments. Schools need to have safety plans in place that safeguard students from being harassed in any manner that hinders their opportunities for a safe and equitable education.

The transition from middle school to high school is critical in setting the stage for the increased likelihood of freshman success or failure. Educators and parents must be vigilant on their watch to ensure that strategies are in place that will ensure student success and safety.

RESEARCH

According to the research of Hertzog and Morgan (1999), schools that implement five or more transition activities ensure a more successful transition experience for students. This research suggests schools develop transition activities under the five areas of curriculum, safety/discipline, facilities, teachers and counselors, and general.

Schools that have a systemic process for informing parents of the increase in academic rigor from middle school to high school, the differences in expectations and policies governing student safety, familiarizing students with the new facility, and information on support services can create increased opportunities for a seamless and successful transition to occur.

Statistics from the Center from the National High School Center revealed students who miss on the average twenty days of school or more are at risk of being retained, statistics that lead to increased drop-out rates (Kennelly and Monrad, 2007). The reasons behind students with high absenteeism like Jonathan can be deeper than failing grades. The U.S. Department of Education and U.S. Department of Health and Human Services provide alarming data on bullying and harassment in today's schools.

Higher absenteeism rates prevail in schools where harassment and bullying are reported in greater numbers (Balfanz and Byrnes, 2012). One in three students will be harassed in today's schools (Roberts, Zhang, Truman, and Snyder, 2010). This same research revealed harassment as one of the leading causes of student absenteeism and one of the main reasons students drop out of school. Plain and simple, harassment is connected to poor academic performance, high absenteeism, and increased drop-out rates.

Schools must have strategic plans in place to familiarize students with the new buildings they enter into to ensure a safe and orderly journey. Schools must develop clearly defined safety plans and implement processes for building teacher/student relationships such as advisor and mentoring programs. Programs should involve providing parent activities that help prepare their children for the changes ahead during this transition. Schools that have in place such plans step in the right direction toward eradicating the lifetime of pain, suffering, and loss experienced by students like Jonathan.

INTERVENTIONS

What could have been done to help Jonathan during the transition from middle school to high school? Did the high school teachers receiving Jonathan really know him? Did the middle school teachers "letting go" of Jonathan inform the high school teachers of students like Jonathan who were brilliant, shy, and underdeveloped? Did the middle school and high school team up to host a tour of the high school?

Did either school have a parent information session on listening to the needs of their child, informing parents of the resources available to help their child in the transition to the high school, familiarizing students on the hot spots to avoid when possible or how to respond when things are going in a non-desired direction? What is the high school safety plan? What is the plan for supervising bathrooms?

Too many high schools feel they do not need to monitor students in the bathroom like the elementary teachers do . . . they are high school kids, young adults. Why was Jonathan not connected to anyone where he felt comfortable enough to go to them and explain what happened?

The following are examples of activities that any school can implement to better ensure student success during periods of transition. Let us work together; middle schools collaborating with high schools, parents collaborating with teachers, and teachers collaborating with teachers from the feeder schools to ensure that we never lose another child like Jonathan.

How many activities does your school implement? What other transition activities can you add to the list?

1. High school freshman mentor program.
2. Grade eight tour of the high school.
3. Middle school/high school teacher swap for a day in order to familiarize high school teachers with incoming grade eight students. This encounter allows teachers and students to put a face with a name, thereby easing the move to the high school.
4. Does the high school counselor meet with grade eight students to inform them of the high school policies on harassment, safety, and reporting any inappropriate behavior?
5. Does your high school host a parent orientation for grade nine students and parents entering the high school?

6. When a student begins to demonstrate a downward spiral in grades, an increase in absenteeism, and perhaps an increase in behavior incidences, do we have, as a school family, a plan for "response to intervention"?
7. What defines a school culture? Do teachers really know the students? Do educators have an individual growth plan on each student where they know their academic, attendance, and behavioral history that includes the student's goals, dreams, and aspirations? Do educators periodically meet with students in charting the course that will help these dreams become a reality?
8. Other.

REFERENCES

Balfanz, R., and Byrnes, V. (2012, May). The importance of being in school: A report on absenteeism in the nation's public schools. Retrieved from http://new.every1graduates.org/wp-content/uploads/2012/05/FINALChronicAbsenteeism-Report_May16.pdf.

Hertzog, C. J., and Morgan, P. L. (1999). Making the transition from middle level to high school. *High School Magazine*, 6(4), 26–30.

Kennelly, L., and Monrad, M. (2007, October). Approaches to dropout prevention: Heeding early warning signs with appropriate interventions. Retrieved from https://files.eric.ed.gov/fulltext/ED499009.pdf.

Roberts, S., Zhang, J., Truman, J., & Snyder, T. (2010, November). Indicators of school crime and safety: 2000. In *Bureau of Justice Statistics*. Retrieved from http://bjs.ojp.usdoj.gov/content/pub/pdf/iscs10.pdf.

2

THEY CALLED HIM STINKY

As educators, we analyze why student grades many times begin to plummet as this age learner enters high school. Districts are keenly aware of freshman failure rates that plague high schools across the nation. Grade nine posts the largest failure rates in high schools across the country (George and McEwin, 1999). High schools blame middle schools, parents blame teachers . . . and the blame game goes round and round. Have educators defined the causes to the problem of freshman failures and dropout statistics? The issue is multi-faceted, somewhat simple to detect but complex to solve.

The emotional intelligence of students and teachers is one issue that must be addressed in the transition to high school. Teachers teach children—not just content. Parents and educators must work together to develop strategies that start from the inside out in addressing student needs in order to ensure both success in high school and a successful transition to the high school. High school kids are "little kids in big people bodies." Educators and parents all too often forget the fragility of the inner child of a high-school age student, especially freshman.

Maslow's hierarchy of needs informs us of the critical nature of having our basic needs met before we are capable of learning. In addition, a student's self-esteem cannot be overlooked when finding solutions to why students skip school, drop-out altogeth-

er, have low performance, or, even worse, complete suicide at alarming rates during this time of their growth and development.

VIGNETTE

Sammy lived with his mom and his mom's boyfriend. Three other siblings joined the family unit. Each of the kids had the same mom but different dads. They shared a two-bedroom apartment. Four kids slept in the same room, two to a bed. Sammy was a ninth grader sharing a twin bed with his little three-year-old brother, Freddie. Freddie had kidney infections rather frequently that caused him to wet the bed often. No matter how Sammy worked on his personal hygiene, he smelled like urine. Water bills often went unpaid and the lack of running water for showers became a challenge for both daily hygiene and washing clothes.

Kids complained to teachers about Sammy. They pleaded, "Please, move him away from me!" On the bus, like a line from the movie Forest Gump, when Sammy went to sit in a seat with only one student, the student quickly responded with, "This seat's taken." Sammy moved to the back of the bus, only to sit alone and watch as no one ever joined the kid that said the seat was taken.

In math class, even the teacher shunned Sammy. She went out of her way to spend more time providing assistance to kids on the other side of the room away from where Sammy's desk was. (Makes you wonder why she assigned Sammy a seat in the last row along the wall.) If the truth be known, she too went to the principal asking that Sammy be moved out of her class stating she was nauseated at the stench.

Just a few years earlier in middle school Sammy actually excelled in math. Then things changed. Dad lost his job, the drinking began, the abuse started, a divorce followed, and the boyfriends came to the trailer in droves.

Sammy needed help in math that was now referred to as pre-algebra. It wasn't that he couldn't do the math; it was just that he had a hard time concentrating on the teacher's instruction because of the comments and gestures by his classmates making fun of his body odor. To raise his hand and ask for help just called more attention to himself, so he kept to himself and tried to figure it out on his own. He fell further behind in his work.

Not only did Sammy smell, but he was hungry too. He went to bed at night ravenous, anxious to wolf down his free breakfast and lunch the next day at school. There were times at night as he lay in bed with Freddie that it seemed like all he could think about was food: not math, not even the hurtful comments from kids . . . just food.

It became more comfortable for Sammy to skip school and hang out at the local pool hall rather than face the ridicule from his peers day after day in school. His reputation at school earned him the nickname "Stinky." At the pool hall he earned a name for himself as a pool shark. This reputation afforded him the one thing positive in his life worth working on that gave him recognition. Sammy came to realize, however, there was not a lot of demand for a job as a pool shark.

Eventually Sammy became a regular no show at school and then, finally, a drop-out statistic. Sammy took to scavenging for food scraps in the dumpster behind the pool hall.

Sammy had many needs that were not being met. He needed something to feel good about. Sammy needed math, he needed to be in school, and he needed help with his basic need for food and shelter before he could learn what we needed to have him learn in school.

RESEARCH

There are a myriad number of reasons students drop out of school. Lack of self-esteem is one reason students leave school as soon as they come of age and are able to self-withdraw from school (McNeal, 1997). A growing number of students and parents are choosing to homeschool students (Lips and Feinberg, 2009). If kids do not fit in, parents in alarming numbers elect to create their own schools or homeschool. These options are many times less than desirable, taught by less than qualified, uncertified people.

What can schools intentionally do to build student esteem? Counselors can create and implement quality advisory programs that equip students with effective coping skills (Osofsky, Sinner, and Wolk, 2003). Teachers can be assigned to a student as a mentor targeting at-risk youth: those with high absenteeism and failing grades that live in high poverty. Counselors can provide options to students who have less resources at home to help them come to school clean, ready to concentrate on school work rather than on their body odor and body image.

How many students in America go to school hungry? According to a 2012 article (Child Hunger in America: Understanding the Issue), sixteen million children experience hunger in a given year. The number of U.S. households without running water is over one and a half million (Gasteyer and Vaswani, 2004). Many children like Sammy may not have the means of showering daily. What alternatives do schools offer these students? In these challenging and difficult economic times, many families are falling further into lower poverty levels while more students are entering poverty for the first time due to situational poverty (Payne, 1996).

Teachers and school leaders must be vigilant on their watch to identify the Sammys of the world. Families and students thrust into situational poverty may find it even harder to admit what they need before the student is in dire trouble.

INTERVENTIONS

What options could schools create to help students like Sammy?

1. Provide private shower opportunities to these students. Contact community businesses, such as hotels, grocery stores, and dentists, to donate shampoo, soap, deodorant, toothbrushes, and toothpaste, and so forth, to help students with personal hygiene items.

2. Does your school have a family resource center where families in need can get food items, clean clothing, and toiletries?
3. Does your school make home visits to identify students like Sammy? Do social services need to get involved? What other community services could help Sammy and his family during this difficult time?
4. Ever request a parent conference? Perhaps there is an underlying health issue causing the body odor that had either gone undetected or untreated?
5. Do you have an advisory program where students can role play situational issues such as the one Sammy experienced and have the students talk about how they would react in these situations? Work with students on character education improving their empathy for others. Do students really think Sammy liked being in the situation where he knew he smelled? Did he like being made fun of? How could educators better handle the next situation with a student like Sammy?
6. Other.

REFERENCES

Child hunger in America: Understanding the issue. (2012). In *ConAgra Foods Foundation nourish today flourish tomorrow*. Retrieved from http://www.conagrafoodsfoundation.org/child-hunger/child-hunger-in-America.jsp.

Gasteyer, S., and Vaswani, R. T. (2004). Still living without the basics in the 21st century: Analyzing the availability of water sanitation services in the United States. Retrieved from http://www.win-water.org/reports/RCAP_full_final.pdf.

George, P., and McEwin, C. (1999). High schools for a new century: Why is the high school changing? *NASSP Bulletin*, *83*(606), 10–24.

Lips, D., and Feinberg, E. (2009, September). Homeschooling: The sleeping giant of America [Electronic version]. *USA Today Magazine*, *138*(2772), 22–24.

McNeal, R. B. (1997, March). High school dropouts: A closer examination of school effects [Electronic version]. *Social Science Quarterly*, *78*(1), 209–22.

Osofsky, D., Sinner, G., and Wolk, D. (2003). Changing systems to personalize learning: The power of advisories. In *The Education Alliance at Brown University*. Retrieved from https://www.brown.edu/academics/education-alliance/sites/brown.edu.academics.education-alliance/files/publications/thepower.pdf.

Payne, R. K. (1996). *A framework for understanding poverty*. Highlands, TX: aha! Process, Inc.

U.S. Department of Commerce. (2012, September 12). Poverty. In *United States Census Bureau*. Retrieved from http://www.census.gov/hhes/www/poverty/about/overview/index.html.

3

LOCKER ROOM HORROR STORIES

Too big, too little, too flat, too fat. The locker room can make students hate physical education and make them want to skip gym class. Educators may define the problem as kids today are lazy, and girls are too afraid to engage in activity for fear of breaking a fingernail. But the problem may be the educators that do not understand, respect, or honor the social and developmental stages of young adolescents, especially incoming ninth graders.

Most students entering grade nine are fourteen to fifteen years of age. Next to infancy, research informs us that during this time, students will go through one of the fastest developmental growth spurts the human body will experience in a lifetime. On an average, these adolescent students grow three to five inches in height in a year. Weight will begin to fluctuate as hormones kick in. Private parts for both sexes develop . . . or not . . . that can make students the envy of the class or the brunt of all jokes. Nicknames can be given to those who are the target of such careless acts of taunting that stick with them forever.

In time, these very students may be proud of their size and physical maturity, but during this critical time when students struggle to accept who and what they are, it can be a living hell.

VIGNETTE

Tim was the high school freshman team quarterback. Popular and handsome, he was the envy of all the boys and his attention was sought after by all of the girls. One would think he had it made, but no one asked him. Tim's private parts were well developed. Even his friends made fun of him, giving him (they thought) bragging rights. But inside, Tim hated his body. He went along with the jokes. Tim even laughed at himself to hide the hurt. He resented the fact that the school did not provide a private place in the locker room where he could go and change clothes without the fear of ridicule and being under the watchful eye of his classmates.

Tim started acting up in gym so he would be removed from the day's lesson. This allowed Tim to be sent to the locker room earlier than the other students so he could dress before the others came in. As a result, Tim's grade in class became negatively impacted due to his inappropriate behavior and early exodus from class participation.

Barb was overweight. In dressing out for PE, the uniforms were not very flattering to a girl her size. The uniforms even accented her heavy thighs and hips. Undressing with all the skinny cheerleaders in her class made her cringe. She was mortified when others glanced at the size 16 tag in her slacks and her 2X sweaters. She also heard comments about her body odor.

Little did her classmates know that Barb lived in poverty. Having an extra can of deodorant to take to school for her private personal use was not going to happen. Toiletries the family did have were to be shared among the many family members at home.

Barb began to skip class and withdraw to the sidelines where she could fade into the bleachers. She preferred a lowered grade for not engaging in the required activities over being a social outcast due to sweaty clothes and a smelly body by participating. She wasn't about to take a shower in a gang-type setting either. Her grade was further lowered by not dressing out, occasionally skipping, by not participating and not showering.

Katrina was flat chested. She hated undressing and dressing with others in the tiny locker room. She was painfully private and shy. The locker room was a place she dreaded going. Just thinking about the school day and the approaching PE class made her nauseated.

Teachers many times think kids are faking illnesses just to get out of participating. For some that may be true, but for many, it may be our classroom that is causing the pain and it is the educator's lack of understanding or their inability to respond to the social and developmental needs of the young people entrusted in their care. If teachers would only realize the culture they have created in their classrooms. A negative classroom culture can cause physical harm to students in the form of ulcers and panic attacks, to name a few. The toll of the emotional stress can linger for years.

When kids skip our classes or school we blame the child, but perhaps we need to look in the mirror first. Perhaps it is the negative culture we as educators have created.

RESEARCH

Middle school and freshman students are often referred to as tweeners. These students are in between adolescence and adulthood. Next to early infancy, their bodies are growing at one of the fastest rates in the growth and development cycle (Iannelli, 2010). These years can be both awkward and humiliating as students are powerless in controlling their ability to "grow into their own skin." Some students can grow up to three and a half inches in height a year. Some girls develop a shapely figure while boys experience changes as a result of higher testosterone levels (Iannelli, 2010).

Again, schools that design activities that prepare students for what to expect with their changing bodies help students in the transition from middle school to high school. Schools that involve students in some of the decision making, as in the selection of PE uniforms, create better school cultures that foster a safe and orderly environment conducive to learning.

INTERVENTIONS

1. Take a tour of your locker room facilities. Are there differences in the boys' and girls' locker rooms with regard to cleanliness and privacy? Note the shower facilities and bathroom facilities. Do they demonstrate respect of and for a student's need for privacy?
2. Administer an anonymous student survey to find out how students feel about the locker rooms and the bathrooms. Too many high school teachers remark and believe: "These kids are high school kids now . . . they have to get tough, suck it up, and grow up. Stop being shy about it, get dressed, and get on the field."
3. Too many teachers seem to have forgotten what those nightmarish developmental years were like. Sure, we survived them, but we all carry some little scars we cannot forget. For some students the scars have created a disfiguring of the spirit that lasts a lifetime. Some scars are visible—many lie within the human psyche.
4. Check your school facilities. The true test: If the facilities are not conducive to you as a teacher using them, why would they be ok for our kids?
5. If you require uniforms for PE, take a look at what body builds of the students required to wear them. Is there a better design to be had? The same question should apply to the band and choir uniforms.
6. Take a look at your school furniture. How do the plus-size students look and feel sitting in these? Do you know? Have you asked them? Can we who may be of average or petite builds really relate to the needs of others?

REFERENCES

Hertzog, C. J., and Morgan, P. L. (1999). Making the transition from middle level to high school. *High School Magazine*, 6(4), 26–30.

Iannelli, V. (2010, June 7). The short child: Short children and normal growth. In *About.com*. Retrieved from http://pediatrics.about.com/od/growthanddevelopment/a/510_short_child.htm.

4

CUT—DISCONNECTED—DRIFTING

In the transition from middle school to high school, students who were "top dogs" in school up to this point begin to be "beat out by others" or rather, cut. In elementary and middle school, many students were involved in lots of things. Everything they tried out for they were selected into. They loved school, and they loved being the center of things and in the limelight. For many students that all changed as they transitioned from middle school to high school. Suddenly, freshman classmates from the other feeder schools seemed bigger, faster, better. To a high school kid, the word "cut" can be one of the most dreaded words to hear.

VIGNETTE

Roy played and started center position on the middle school basketball team. He was not tall, but for some reason he was the tallest kid in his eighth-grade class of "runts." Being the tallest in this group left one with little room for bragging as no one was tall. His middle school was one of three schools that fed into the one high school in the district. When it came time for high school freshman tryouts, Roy could tell he would no longer be playing center. There was too much height around him to fill that position. He thought surely he would fill one of the twelve places on the team.

His heart was pounding as he entered the locker room where the team roster was to be posted. He scanned the list four times before he could fathom the realization that he was cut. A month later, he tried out for the academic team. He was cut. Come spring, Roy tried out for the golf team. Again, he was cut. No longer connected to the things he once loved, Roy began his own form of cuts. He began cutting class.

Shelley was a singer who sang in church. She was in middle school chorus and in a special singing group that went around town singing to local community interest groups. Many times Shelley sang solos. Her parents and grandparents always bragged about her voice. It became what she was known for.

As she entered high school, Shelley was in the freshman chorus. (All you had to do to be in the chorus was ask to have chorus on your schedule). She tried out for the elite high school performing group but did not make it! As the year progressed, Shelley hoped the choral director would select her for a solo. She even asked the director if she could sing one. But solos, one by one, were given to others.

The final straw that broke the camel's back came when Shelley tried out for the musical, *My Fair Lady*. She did not get a singing part but she was asked to be a spectator in the backdrop of the Ascot racing scene. Shelley was devastated. She began to be a spectator alright. She went from a happy-go-lucky girl with a bubbly personality to a rather withdrawn character as she faded into the bland school walls around her.

Kids like Roy and Shelley can lose their identity in the transition from middle school to high school. The damage left by students not finding their niche, of not fitting in, can be very difficult to accept. Without the proper interventions in place from home and school in coping with these defeats, it can begin to create a distancing from school.

Kids at this critical crossroad can begin to disconnect from school because there is nothing for them to connect to. Activities these students once associated with that identified who and what they were known for are no longer an option. Schools and parents begin to lose kids because they do not have a way of addressing the needs of these kids who were once involved that now are not.

What about the kids who were never involved? These kids are even at a greater disadvantage and at a greater risk of being lost during the transition from middle school to high school because schools do not provide more opportunities or intentionally plan to connect them to something positive in school.

RESEARCH

Success in school can be linked to a sense of belonging (Ma, 2003). By nature, human beings need to be connected to something. Being a part of something greater than one's self further develops one's identity, fostering positive relationships and interaction with others. Being on a sport team, participating in the band, or becoming a member of the chess club, and so on, are all examples of how students can connect to school.

One should look no further than the research on the positive impact student participation in extracurricular activities has on student success. Research reveals a strong correlation to improved student self-esteem, improved grades, and improved attendance of students who are involved school-related activities (Simoncini and Caltobiono, 2012).

On the downside, students not involved in extracurricular activities as frequently as their grade-level peers suffer more anxiety- and depression-related illnesses (Simoncini and Caltobiono, 2012). Not fitting in, not being a part of a team, a club, the band, a choir, can further isolate some students from others. For some students who were once very active, the envy of others, the star, the pain of not making the "cut" is even more debilitating and detrimental to a student's sense of self-worth (DeBroff, n.d.).

INTERVENTIONS

1. Some athletes blossom later in high school than others. Super star Michael Jordan was cut from his high school team as a junior!
2. What additional programs can schools implement that can continue to improve student skills and keep more students involved and interacting with others? Do you have a before school or after school intramural program? Saturday morning open recreation opportunities? Why do many school coaches guard that sacred basketball, football, or baseball field as if taxpayers were only paying for these facilities for blue chip athletes? School facilities should service all students.
3. Ever think about offering year-round cheerleading clinics? What about having a competition squad and a different squad that cheers for the players on the field?
4. Whether cheering for the girls' or guys' teams on the field or the court, being a cheerleader is about knowing what is happening on the field or court and getting the crowd rallying behind the team. Any student is capable of being a cheerleader. All it really takes is charisma and a good set of lungs. Compared to the high cost of gymnastics or dance lessons, charisma and a good old GO—FIGHT—WIN is cheap!
5. What about offering free lessons before school starts? You might be surprised how many of your faculty play in a band, write poetry, sing at church, clog with a local dance troupe, ballroom dance, or draw. Teachers could showcase their talents while teaching kids at the same time.
6. Create more opportunities for *all* students to get involved in something positive. Being involved and being connected to school and with peers might just be the one thing that makes students want to stay in school and graduate.

REFERENCES

DeBroff, S. (n.d.). The final cut: How to help your child deal with the rejection of not making the team. In *Curious Parent*. Retrieved from http://www.curiousparents.com/Main/xq/asp/article.409sports/qx/article.htm.

Ma, X. (2003, July). Sense of belonging to school: Can schools make a difference? [Electronic version]. *Journal of Educational Research, 96*(6), 340–49.

Simoncini, K., and Caltobiono, N. (2012, September). Young school-aged children's behavior and their participation in extra-curricular activities [Electronic version]. *Australasian Journal of Early Childhood, 37*(3), 8.

5

PARENTS IN THE TRANSITION

Are you kidding me? Stop making excuses as a parent, as a high school, and as high school teachers about parental involvement. Collaborate with parents to get more parents in our high schools. Love for children can be expressed in many ways. Being there for them and being with them every step of the journey builds a sense of security that is a huge expression of love and support.

When students feel parental and adult presence in their lives by attending their school activities and meeting with teachers, high school students come to know they can depend on the adults in their lives. Students come to know the adults are there for them. Students know they can take positive risks because they have parental support and backing.

Designing parental involvement programs in schools should not be limited to elementary and middle schools. High schools must not lose years of collaborative partnerships with parent participation in our schools in the transition to the high school. Some high school teachers and parents think "it is time to let go." But is it?

VIGNETTE

Adam was an active kid. He loved school and participated in a multitude of extracurricular activities. Adam's parents never missed an event Adam participated in. You could feel the sense of pride from his parents as they watched him score the winning game point or flub his lines in a school play. If practice was over at 5:00 p.m., they were there to pick him up at 5:00 p.m. Adam's parents attended any and all parent conferences. If one would ask "why" because he was already an A/B student, perhaps in part it was because they were so involved.

Things never changed as he moved from middle school to high school. His parents were equally as active in the transition to the high school. If the truth be known, upon leaving high school for college, his parents were still present at soccer games and events that were important to him. They even inquired regularly about his grades by calling him at college every Sunday night without fail.

Tammie was not an athlete, not a singer, nor an artist. She liked school but she was rather shy, a bit of a loner, an avid reader. The school created a schedule for parent conferences. Her mom (a single parent) attended every one. Not many high school parents attended these planned events. In a meeting with the school counselor, Tammie was complimented on her mom's visibility at school. Tammie commented that her mom was the greatest. She said her mom stayed on top of things and was not one to wait until there was a problem. Tammie shared that one of her mom's favorite sayings is, "Better to be proactive than reactive."

Once you become a parent, being a parent is not optional. Get involved. Stay involved. You do not stop being a parent when your child moves from middle to high school. Do not put on the brakes in your participation and involvement in your young adult's school. Work with your child's high school to develop and participate in activities. Remember, high schools kids are just "little kids in big people bodies." Parents need to be present in this critical transition to high school.

When high school kids say they do not want their parents at school, they are really saying "not if other parents don't come to school." Parents sometimes take the easy way out in looking at high school kids. On one hand, parents like the fact that they do not have to continue to be in close contact with the school. Some parents like that these students can even drive to school. Students become more independent as they grow older. However, far too many parents "pull out too quickly" with each advancing transition.

Kids really do want parents there but they are afraid that it looks immature on their part. Students say they do not want you in the school, but they do. The high school years lay the foundation for life. Be in them!

To a fault, high school teachers many times express that at this level, parents need to back off and let the student take charge. This can be a dangerous time of complacency. Teacher attitudes about parental involvement can many times mask the fact that high school teachers simply do not want to have to show up for or be involved in one more parent conference or parent activity.

We must not forget that schooling today is *not* what it was forty years ago. Many students do not have the parents that laid the strong foundation many of us were afforded. There is no handbook on how to be a parent. Schools can help a great deal in providing lessons to be shared with parents in steering kids in the right direction. Keep these parent/school collaborative partnerships alive!

RESEARCH

Billman (2004) explains how effective schools have strong parental involvement programs (p. 25 para). Research exists on the importance of parental involvement in higher performing schools (Executive Summary, What Worked?). Communication between home and school can be strengthened with the support of active parent groups (Blagojevich, 2004).

Parental involvement is no longer about volunteering to bring cupcakes and take tickets at a ballgame. With high-stakes accountability and the increasing demands for all students to be career and college ready, parents must stay and be connected to their child's school in a more meaningful way. It is important that parents know the teachers and school leaders, know the curriculum expectations, and know the support services available to help their child to be career and college ready (Davis, 2000).

INTERVENTIONS

1. What systemic process is in place at your school to help parents help their student/child in the transition from the middle school to the high school? People say kids no longer want their parents hanging around at school. We are providing an injustice with a total "hands off approach." Students are not suddenly grown up just because they walk through the high school door. Keep parents involved in their kid's schooling. How many activities below does your school have in place?

   - Host a parent orientation session in the move from middle school to high school. Provide an informative session that describes the changes and expectations that are a normal part of this transition. Share expectations for grades, behavior, interventions, and extra support and counseling support resources, and so on.
   - Schedule periodic parent meetings: Donuts for Dads, Muffins for Moms, etc. Schedule open forums to hear parent questions and concerns to improve communication from school to home.
   - Develop a "Parent Newsletter" informing parents of how to get involved or stay involved in their child's schooling that also informs parents of upcoming events. (Put an energetic parent who is technology savvy in the development of this newsletter.)
   - Develop a fun night with parents: Develop an "Arts Night," "Sports Night," and so on, where things are not

always academic focused but focused on the arts or health and wellness topics. These types of events are less threatening to parents who have limited education attainment backgrounds. These events build trust in the school and encourage involvement.
- What other ideas can you generate?

REFERENCES

Billman, P. (2004, December). Mission possible: Achieving and maintaining academic improvement. *NIU Outreach*, 1–59.

Blagojevich, R. R. (2004). School/home communication: Using technology to enhance parental involvement. A project for the Illinois Century Network and Governor Rod R Blagojevich [Electronic version]. *Center for the Study of Education Policy*, 100.

Davis, D. (2000, June). Supporting parent, family, and community involvement in your school. Retrieved from http://www.pacer.org/mpc/pdf/titleipip/SupportingInvolvement_article.pdf.

6

DAD'S IN JAIL, MOM'S ALWAYS HIGH, AND I LIVE WITH MY GRANDPARENTS

Let's face it . . . life presents us with lots of transitions that are scary. Remember what it was like to leave home and enter kindergarten? How about that move from half-day kindergarten to first grade? Transitioning from grade five at the elementary school to that huge middle school was a doozy too!

The transition from middle school to high school is even more frightening. As students advance each grade in school, kids are less likely to share their inner fears and concerns and therefore less likely to ask for help or guidance in the transition. With every transition the new environment usually gets bigger. Personal relationships with teachers that really know you become lessened. Students can become more of a number than a name. It is here where students can become "lost in transition." It is here where teachers begin to know less and less of "where a child is from" and the obstacles they may face daily just to get to school.

VIGNETTE

Maggie was a precocious ninth grader. She was more advanced than other classmates in many ways and yet more immature in others. She bounced down the halls in an aggressive manner, teetering between and obnoxious adolescence and a young women, a "tweener" if you will. Conversations in the teachers' lounge were dominated by stories of Maggie's escapades. She frequented the principal's office enough that he began to think of her more as his assistant!

Teachers were highly frustrated with Maggie's call outs in class, her lack of attention to her grades, and her obsession with boys! Her behavior by all accounts appeared to be getting worse. Teachers began sending Maggie to the office and out of class, demanding that she be sent to in-school suspension and considered for alternative school.

Not one teacher took the time to go to the counselor's office to peruse Maggie's permanent folder. It was the stuff movies are made of. Maggie's dad was in jail for theft, assault, and sadly, sexual abuse of Maggie and her little sister. Maggie's mom was known around town as a druggie and prostitute, and the children were often left alone to fend for themselves. For the record, grandma was her legal guardian. At seventy-eight years of age, Grandma had little hearing left and she was on disability. Maggie was the one in charge.

Maggie many times assumed the role of caregiver to both her younger sibling and Grandma. Under the circumstances, Maggie did remarkably well getting herself and her sister up each morning, fed, and ready for school. Looking at attendance records, neither of the girls missed much school. If the truth be known, it was home the kids were running away from and the school they were running to. School was their lifeline, their safe haven. School was a place that they could be just little girls. The inappropriate behavior at school garnered Maggie the attention from adults she so longed for.

Maggie's flaunting of herself toward boys in the class was her way of trying to gain a sense of status among her classmates. She was a pretty good athlete back in middle school, but with mom always strung out and dad in jail . . . no one could shuttle her to and from practices and games. She had a pretty good voice too. But again, participation in after school events was no longer an option for her. Maggie's overconfident demeanor masked her true lack of self-esteem. Maggie was in survival mode just to have her basic needs met of food and shelter. She lacked as well a real sense of being loved and truly cared for.

Maggie's middle school teachers new Maggie's life story that read like a tragic play. They kept a close eye on her and provided safety nets at every turn. But when the "hand-off" from the middle to high school occurred, no one informed those who would be receiving Maggie of the obstacles she faced.

By Christmas of her freshman year in high school Maggie was in alternative school and pregnant. By March of that same year Maggie quit coming to school. No one knows where Maggie lives anymore. You can almost write the ending of this story.

RESEARCH

Nine percent of students nationally who have parents that are or who have been incarcerated are more likely to become a drop-out statistic compared to their peers that do not share in these same challenges (Crain, n.d.). Today, 42.8 percent of youth are being raised by a grandparent (U.S. Census Bureau, 2005).

Do you know the percentage of students in your school with incarcerated parents? Children exposed to excessive alcohol and drug use in the home are four times more likely to become users themselves (Family matters: Substance abuse and the American family, 2005). Drug and alcohol use negatively impacts academic performance, drop-out statistics, attendance, and increased behavior incidences (Pergamit, Huang, and Lane, 2001).

INTERVENTIONS

1. Implement counseling programs that connect students who live in homes mired by addictive behaviors to support groups or intervention groups.
2. Be aware of the number of students in your school being raised by a grandparent. This is not always a negative thing

and in fact, in most situations a positive one. But for some, the generational differences and health issues of the grandparent further exacerbates the problems associated with the growth and development of a high school age student. Work intentionally as a school family to provide the student's family with social service resources and supports they need for the student to be successful.
3. Develop a mentoring program in your school. Get local business leaders to "adopt" an identified at-risk youth and serve as a role model to help the student make proper life style choices and help them in setting attainable goals.
4. Educators can identify the list of students headed down the wrong path in school that will negatively impact them negative for a lifetime. Teachers can identify these students as early as middle school, perhaps even in elementary school. Can your staff generate a list of these students in each grade? Add to the list the support services the school is providing these students. Is there more we could do? What other options are available?

REFERENCES

Crain, C. (n.d.). Children of offenders and the cycle of intergenerational incarceration. In *TDCJ Go Kids*. Retrieved from http://www.aca.org/fileupload/177/ahaidar/Crain.pdf.

Family matters: Substance abuse and the American family. (2005, March). In *The CASA White Paper*. Retrieved from http://www.casacolumbia.org/articlefiles/380-Family%20Matters.pdf.

Pergamit, M., Huang, L., and Lane, J. (2001, August). *National Opinion Research Center*. Retrieved from http://aspe.hhs.gov/hsp/riskybehav01/chapt2.htm.

U.S. Census Bureau. (2005). Percent of grandparent responsible for their grandchildren: 2005—United States—county by state; and for Puerto Rico Universe: Grandparents living with own grandchildren less than 18 years. Retrieved from http://factfinder2.census.gov/faces/tableservices/jsf/pages/productview.xhtml?pid=ACS_05_EST_GCT1001.US05PR&prodType=table.

7

ABOVE HIS RAISIN'

In Appalachian culture, there is a saying that many parents fear their child will "get above their raisin'" the more educated they become. Some parents therefore do not value higher levels of educational attainment.

The real fear perhaps lies in not that the child will attain more of an education than the parent, but rather, the child will forget from where they came and leave home for good. Education does open the eyes and minds of young adults, no doubt. But parents need to encourage and not stifle the fulfillment and self-actualization that comes with expanding one's way of thinking called learning that enables one to grow and become all that one is capable of becoming.

There are two precious gifts we can give our children: one is roots, the other is wings. Parents need to be encouraged to give kids the gift of an education that gives flight to their dreams, that gives them wings to fly high with. If parents have done a good job at parenting, kids may fly away and soar, but the strong roots will always keep them connected to "from where they came" and bring them home again.

VIGNETTE

Jimmy noticed high school counselors were a lot different than they were back in middle school. At the high school, counselors held individual and group sessions with students with an intense focus on career counseling. Counselors and teachers were always scheduling ACT prep activities and remediation sessions. Students were constantly administered tests to improve ACT scores with the goal of improving opportunities to go to college. Jimmy often thought all of this was a bunch of "bull," and so did his parents. Jimmy knew what he wanted to do. He was going to work in the coal mines, just like his daddy and his grandpappy before him.

During his freshman year in high school, Jimmy found himself headed to one of those dreaded assemblies. Along with his 248 other freshman classmates, he was herded down the hallway to the gym. Upon entering the gym, Jimmy was quickly guided to a roundtable session where he took a career inventory test.

He thought this little exercise was rather comical and a waste of his time to be asked questions like, "Do you like working outdoors? Like working with people? Like speaking in front of groups?" The list of questions seemed endless. Upon finishing, he was then presented with a printout on the results of that inventory. Jimmy never really thought much about things like that, but to his surprise, the test results did rather accurately reveal some things to Jimmy that really made him think.

Jimmy was then shuttled off to another table where some local business leaders talked with the table group about industry jobs, what their businesses had to offer, and the type of education required for certain positions. They talked about "benefits" they offered like health insurance, paying for college classes, retirement, paid sick days, and other things. They even offered a salary scale.

Some jobs paid more than his daddy made in the mines, and some paid less. His dad's salary puffed Jimmy up as he thought "my dad really makes good money . . . and I will too!" Jimmy thought,

"Why pay out for college when I can go right into the mines and make as much if not more than a lot of these positions!"

Jimmy rotated to other tables where folks talked about careers in the health industry, education, the auto industry, technology, chemical engineering, banking, sales, sports management, and so on. The two hours in the gym flew by! Jimmy's mind was racing and his heart was pounding by the time he boarded the bus at the end of the school day! He never imagined all of the options available to him beyond the mines.

Jimmy noticed other things that day that went beyond just what the people at the tables shared. Some of the men and women presenting were dressed in business casual attire, some in suits and ties. Nonetheless, they were all clean. Each seemed to have their hair neatly combed; their fingernails were well manicured, and each had polished shoes.

He particularly noticed among the older recruiters (those about his dad's age) and how they looked much younger than his dad did with far fewer wrinkles. God only knows Jimmy's daddy and grandpappy came home each night looking like raccoons. Covered in coal from head to foot they were dog dead tired, hacking and coughing to clear their lungs from the day's coal dust.

Jimmy wondered, "What will my dad and gramps have to say when I share with them what I learned about today at school and how it made me think of a future beyond the coal mines?" So many things were running through Jimmy's mind. *Maybe I could be in sports medicine*, he thought. *I love sports! That test said I have high verbal skills. Perhaps I could be a sports newscaster or better yet, an announcer for a major league team on TV! Perhaps I am meant to be a teacher?*

Conversation at home that evening went pretty much as Jimmy feared. Mom starting crying at the thought of Jimmy leaving his hometown to become one of those "high falooten" college-educated city slickers who think they are better than everyone else. Gramps chimed in, "If workin' in the mines was good enough for this family for generations . . . then it ought to be good enough for you." (No one brought up the discussion the family had at the dinner table a few weeks earlier about how the mines are shutting down and what will this community look like in ten years when everyone leaves because the demand for coal's gone.)

At this point Jimmy faced a dilemma: continue to expand his thinking, expand his self-actualization in understanding his talents, his skills, and what he wished to do for the rest of his life to have a better life, or succumb to the pressures of his family and generational thinking that, left unquestioned, could lead to generational poverty.

Jimmy started thinking about what he could to do to prepare for either option: head to college or off to the mines. He began taking more advanced classes. He started talking with the school counselors about dual credit courses offered at the upper grades and what he needed to do to get in those.

Who would have imagined how one transition activity at the high school, the freshman career fair, would change Jimmy's life?

Schools many times do not realize the power of one activity, the power of each day, and the power in what educators do and say daily in our schools that literally change lives. Jimmy now had a vision of what his choices were and what could be . . . and he wanted to be ready for all of them.

RESEARCH

The saying goes "If you don't know where you are going, every road will lead you there." Too many high school students wander aimlessly through their high school years. As students transition to high school, it is not too late to begin teaching students the value of goal setting and it is not too early to begin working with students on setting career goals.

Twenty-first-century schools are being challenged to ensure *all* students leaving our high schools are career and college ready. For students to be competitive in the twenty-first century, the standard level of educational attainment no longer rests with a mere high school diploma. The new normal is for all students to attain an associate degree and beyond. Whether one's career path requires a vocation or an education, students must become certified and skilled in order to lead a successful and productive life.

INTERVENTIONS

1. Does your high school offer dual credit opportunities? If not, what has to happen to get this in place in your school?
2. Do you have apprenticeships and mentoring programs in collaboration with local business community leaders?
3. Do you host various seminars/meetings with parents sharing the importance of advancing one's education? Parents who have never attended college do not know how to navigate this system. Many parents do not know how to help their child through the mounds of paperwork required to apply for college and/or scholarships. Overwhelmed by the process, they revert to encouraging their child to get out of high school and get that good job in the mines, the tobacco fields, and the factories familiar to them. Discuss processes in place in your school or processes you could develop to help parents help their children become college and career ready.
4. What can schools do to expand the thinking of parents who fear their kids will leave the town they have been raised in (even when the town as little job opportunity for them)? Have you ever arranged for students to attend a Chamber of Commerce meeting with the movers and shakers of the community to dream of "what the town could become"?
5. Ever think of having high school students conduct research about what the town has to offer, the location, the economic development, and how to start a business? Let them design a plan. Ever think of having high school kids explore careers in architectural design, landscaping, rock wall building, and so on, and use those skills to design and revitalize a community park? These ideas can create job opportunities for students or perhaps spark a career interest.

6. How many kids are like Jimmy? Without the help of a knowledgeable mentor, kids like Jimmy could easily live out a self-fulfilling prophecy in never reaching their full potential. Name the kids in your school like Jimmy.

REFERENCES

Bragg, D., and Rudd, C. (2007). *Career pathways, academic performance, and transition to college and careers: The impact of two elect career and technical education (CTE) transition programs on student outcomes.* Champagne, IL: Office of Community College Research and Leadership, University of Illinois at Urbana-Champaign.

Hertzog, C. J., and Morgan, P. L. (1999). Making the transition from middle level to high school. *High School Magazine*, 6(4), 26–30.

8

HOME VISITS

I am more than just a teacher. I am a nurse, sometimes a bus driver, a big brother, a counselor. I even make home visits. I never realized what some kids go home to . . . or what some kids actually called a home . . . until I made home visits.

Most teachers are likely from middle-class means. Many went home to a "Leave it to Beaver" type of family structure that included a mom, a dad, a house with a two-car garage, a few other siblings, and a dog or two.

Today, too many of our students live in places most people would not put a dog in. Teachers need not cripple these kids with compassion in knowing the sad conditions they are from. Rather, the bar for these students needs to remain high to help get them out of this dismal state of being. What needs to change is the collective strategies teachers take to help eliminate these students' barriers to reaching high levels of achievement.

VIGNETTE

Oscar was a quiet kid. He was always a little unkempt, usually late getting to school, later still in getting assignments turned in. Elementary teachers made sure Oscar got extra helpings during breakfast and lunch. The Family Resource Center put canned goods in his backpack on Fridays. Teachers pulled him out of related arts classes to give him the extra help he needed to improve his academic performance.

At Christmas time, schools in the district always had secret angels that teachers bought gifts for. Oscar had been on that list of needy families since kindergarten. All of the four elementary schools in the district were quite familiar with Oscar and his family. They moved from trailer park to trailer park or from various housing projects around town every time rent came due. This made the schools like a revolving door as Oscar entered in and out of the all of the schools within the district.

Principals shared notes on how each year, on the day when the Christmas gifts were delivered from the district, Oscar would skip school. He skipped not because of his excitement to receive the gifts—Oscar was embarrassed to have the school leaders who delivered the presents see the conditions in which he lived.

Oscar always greeted the visitors by springing from an old, rat-infested junk car sitting in the front yard. No administrator ever made it to the front door. Oscar did not want anyone coming inside his house. He was ashamed, embarrassed, and determined to take the gifts in the house on his own. What he really feared was the fact that if officials knew the deplorable conditions that he lived, he would be taken from the home and placed in foster care.

Transitioning to high school, Oscar for the first time noticed how his clothes were not of the brand name that would make him popular. He had dreams like everyone else but no one knew all of the obstacles he faced. Oscar had no role models at home, and he started to flounder in the transition to high school.

Like the elementary and middle school he transitioned from, the high school teachers seemed to make the effort to understand his struggles. The teachers communicated often and regularly with each other to discuss Oscar's barriers. A system was put in place to help Oscar. High school teachers worked to connect the dots to provide safety nets and services to help Oscar and other students like him as they transitioned to high school.

High school faculty members in general often make comments like "it is time those middle schoolers grow up. They are in high school now. They need to learn how to stand on their own two feet." That is like asking a wheelchair-bound student to stand up on their own two feet. We know they cannot because of "their condition." Educators must realize that many of our students have conditions where they too cannot "bear the weight alone of the things life is asking of them at this stage of growth and development."

Many teachers believe it is their job to teach the core content. And it is. Many think teaching content is what teacher education programs trained them to do. And it is. But it is *not* the only thing. To be called "Teacher," one must understand and reach out to the whole child in order to help students become a whole person. Should we as a society *have* to deal with these personal issues before we can teach? In a perfect world, perhaps that is not our job. But, it is what it is. Life is not perfect and if not *us*, then *who* will be the lifeline for these students?

For many needy and seemingly hopeless students that enter our classrooms, teachers are their last hope for a brighter tomorrow. It is imperative that high school teachers connect with middle school teachers. Teachers need to know the special needs of *all* children during periods of transition to the new environment and not just the needs of special education students. Schools that develop transition programs can better assist students to be more successful on their journey through school.

RESEARCH

There is a saying, "To teach me you must know me first." Educators need to know their students, where they are from, where they live, and what they aspire to become. If a student's roots are not well planted, it is like building a house on a weak foundation. Educators must be prepared to help lay a strong foundation. If educators do not know where a student is going toward a career goal, it is likely the student will flounder. If teachers know a student's career goals, they can develop individual learning plans and determine what course of action to take in monitoring student progress for success.

In working collaboratively with middle school teachers, high school teachers can become better informed about the needs of the new students coming to them during the transition and set in motion a set of intervention plans or articulation activities (Mizelle and Irvin, 2000) that create a seamless transition. Advisory programs are one means providing a systemic process that allows teachers to know students on a personal level therefore creating a better opportunity to help students in a more intentional way.

INTERVENTIONS

Upon researching middle school to high school transition activities, how many activities could be developed and implemented collaboratively between the middle school and high school in your district to ensure greater success in high school? The research of Hertzog and Morgan (1999) and a study by Christian (2011) provides a framework for discussion on what schools can do.

1. Our school makes home visits to *all* students.
2. Our school counseling program has a systemic plan for connecting "at-risk" students to support systems.
3. Our school has an advisory program in place where a small number of students are assigned to a teacher who knows the student's cumulative folder information: where the child has been, career goals, and interests.
4. Our school keeps an individual evaluation plan on each student. The plan includes career interest surveys, extracurricular activity participation, and behavior and academic reports.
5. Our school has a system in place that provides timely intervention strategies to students who are struggling.
6. When our school realizes a student's family life has obstacles in providing the basic needs of living a happy, healthy life,

there is a system that immediately connects the student and the family to the proper support services.
7. Our middle school collaborates often and regularly with the high school to discuss incoming freshman.
8. Other.

REFERENCES

Christian, C. (2011). An investigation of a middle-high school system as a learning organization during the implementation of a grade eight to grade nine transition program. *Electronic Thesis and Dissertations*. Retrieved from https://doi.org/10.18297/etd/250.

Hertzog, C. J., and Morgan, P. L. (1998). Breaking the barriers between middle school and high school: Developing a transition team for student success. *NASSP Bulletin*, *82*(597), 94–98.

Mizelle, N., and Irvin, J. (2000). Transition from middle school into high school. *Middle School Journal*, *31*(5), 57–71.

9

DUAL CREDIT, APPRENTICESHIPS, CAREER ACADEMIES

What do I want to be when I grow up? That is the question many students ask as they enter high school.

Many schools across the nation are structured in the same manner that their parents grew up in. Our middle schools and high schools operate for the most part as they have for the past fifty years. The questions educators must ask is, "Are we preparing kids for the twenty-first century? Are we leading kids to self-actualization where they become independent learners who can solve problems and think creatively?" "Are today's students flexible and able to adapt and respond to situations they are presented with in any given moment with competence?" "Are schools developing students into team players?"

VIGNETTE

Madeline was always a bright child. Her parents started reading to her early in life. The family traveled a great deal, and these experiences exposed Madeline to diverse cultures. Her vocabulary was more advanced than that of her grade level peers. By the end of grade eight she was in the ninety-ninth percentile and distinguished on most state and national exams she took. She had a 4.0 GPA.

Middle school teachers did not know how to handle Madeline as an advanced student. The teachers helped develop her leadership skills by having her work with students who were not quite on grade level. These types of activities benefit gifted students, to a point. But excelling students like Madeline need nourishment, rigorous work, and higher standards in order to reach their highest levels of potential.

The high school graduated Madeline's older brother four years earlier. He too was a gifted outlier. But unlike the middle school, the high school teachers collaborated regularly to meet his needs as an advanced student. This time they vowed to be even more prepared for Madeline and students like her as she transitioned to the high school.

In the middle of Madeline's grade eight year, high school freshman teachers scheduled regular meetings with the grade eight teachers to gather data on all the advanced students including Madeline that would be transitioning to the high school in less than nine months. The teachers analyzed grades, state assessments, diagnostic assessments, and the leadership skills of each of these students.

The high school teachers worked with the middle school teachers to administer a career interest survey in order to predetermine the budding talents and interests of these advanced students. Grade eight excelling students were then assigned a high school teacher mentor who made arrangements for these students to participate in career apprenticeships during their freshman year in high school that matched their interests.

During the second semester of grade eight, the high school teachers allowed advanced eighth-grade students to enter an online high school Spanish class. In addition, high school gifted students started a club called the Innovators Club. The high school students invited identified grade eight middle school students to be a part of their after school club. The club met regularly to share shorts stories and poems the students had written. Artwork and sculptures developed by the students were also shared along with innovative projects students were working on.

The club had a faculty sponsor and became a "think tank" of creativity and energy. In time, the students shared their struggles with being "different" and how they managed their talents in and out of school with peers, teachers, and parents. Many grade eight students expressed how the club and interactions with high school students like them helped them to become more confident with who they were and how it made the transition to the high school easier. They no longer tried to play down their intelligence but were proud of their talents. For once it was okay and cool to be smart!

RESEARCH

Educators can help gifted students reach their fullest potential with some additional effort and varied teaching strategies. According to Tomlinson (1999), teachers must be prepared to address the needs of all students who come to us, including students with advanced skills and knowledge through differentiation of instruction. Learning centers, tiered activities, compacting, inquiry, and problem-based learning activities are just of the few of the many ways teachers can help excelling students attain greater depths of knowledge. McCook (2006) notes schools must develop response to intervention plans. These plans are not limited to struggling learners.

Teachers need to respond and intervene when excelling kids are in a plateau. If gifted students are not moving forward, they are in fact, moving backward. Educators demonstrate professionalism at the highest degree when they demonstrate authentic interactions as they collaborate and communicate as a common practice (Fullan and Hargreaves,1996). The collaborative efforts of middle school and high school staff can ease the transition for advanced students when strong communication plans are in place between the middle school and high school in order for teachers to plan ahead for incoming freshman with advanced skills.

INTERVENTIONS

1. Identify and discuss the transition activities this high school had in place.
2. How many "Withit" high school transition activities could be replicated in your school?
3. List the transition activities currently in place in your school for incoming freshman.
4. What cost (if any) would be associated with developing and implementing transition activities in schools?
5. Can you name and claim the "gifted" identified students in your classroom? What alternative assignments and options do you intentional plan to take these students to the next level?

It is not just about giving gifted students more problems or having them complete things faster. It is about rigor; it is about depth of learning and inquiry. In table groups, discuss things you have done to extend the thinking of the gifted and talented in your school.

REFERENCES

Fullan, M., and Hargreaves, A. (1996). *What's worth fighting for in your school?* New York: Teachers College Press.

McCook, J. (2006). *The RTI guide: Developing and implementing a model in your schools*. Horsham: LRP Publications

Tomlinson, C. A. (1999). *The differentiated classroom: responding to the needs of all learners.* Alexandria, VA: Association for Supervision and Curriculum Development.

10

DOES ANYBODY HEAR ME? DOES ANYBODY SEE ME? DOES ANYBODY CARE?

People, no matter what age, feel a need to connect to something. Kids that do not have something positive to connect to in school, like sports, often turn to less than desirable role models to emulate. Keeping kids busy and involved in school-sponsored events such as sports, band, choir, or clubs can be the "make or break" experience of a student's secondary school journey.

As students transition from middle school to high school, it is so important that teachers, parents, and school administrators work together to get students involved and affiliated with some part of the school organization whether it be a team or a club. Fewer drop-outs are reported in schools that work to provide opportunities for students to be associated with something positive. Many schools intentionally create a school culture where teachers work together to get all *kids on the roster of something.*

VIGNETTE

Hedra was a chubby, awkward, unassuming eighth grader. She wore glasses, struggled with blemishes, and was painfully shy.

Sports and Hedra went together like oil and water. She would have been the last person connected to a sports team.

Valley High was a grade seven to twelve school. High school teachers had the advantage of knowing many of the middle school students before they entered the high school ranks. The high school girls' basketball coach, Coach Jones, saw something different in Hedra. He was a hard core physical education teacher and coach. But he knew kids. He noticed Hedra as being a loner in class. He noticed her sitting at a separate table during lunch, and he viewed her often being painfully quiet in the classroom.

One day Coach Jones told Hedra he needed a good manager and how critical that position was to the team. He went on to tell her that position was every bit as important to the success of the team as the leading scorer. He looked Hedra in the eye and said, "I am telling you this, Hedra, because I need a person like you on my team. The team needs you."

Hedra looked back at the coach in shock. She had never been asked to be a part of anything like this; she was even more taken back that she was being invited to join a sport team. That night as she lay in bed, she could not get out of her mind what the coach had said to her that day: "He said he needed me, the team needed me." Hedra for the first time felt that her life had some purpose and that her existence mattered.

Coach Jones explained to Hedra at the first practice that one of her responsibilities was to get the basketballs ready and on the ball rack for practices. As practice began, both the coach and the team noticed Hedra did not just walk over to get a loose ball picked up, she ran at break neck speed to pick them up! By the end of practice she had a better workout than many of the players.

At first the team chuckled at her overzealous behavior in practices and games. But as time went on, her behavior became endearing and invaluable to the team and all who knew her. Team members truly saw Hedra as a critically important, contributing member of the team.

Being a part of this organization changed Hedra's life. The team never knew it, but once Hedra had written a note to Coach Jones telling him that she was contemplating suicide. Of course the coach reported this to the parents, the school counselor, and health officials. Behind the scenes they counseled her and provided her the medical help she needed. Years later, as Hedra prepared to receive her high school sports letter, she whispered in the Coach Jones' ear, "Thanks for saving my life. Being a part of the team was my lifeline. I felt for the first time in my life like I was a part of something special. I no longer felt alone, and I was connected to so many wonderful teammates that came to be my friends."

How many of your students wander aimlessly, disconnected from organizations, school, and others? They may want to come to you and inquire about getting involved, but for various reasons, they shy away. A personal invitation can go a long way in helping students get involved.

As teachers and coaches, educators need to reach out to the quiet, sometimes voiceless students who sit in our classrooms. Especially during the transition from middle school to high school, it is important that students have a sense of belonging. Schools that serve students well provide numerous activities that allow students to be a part of something under the guidance and watchful eye of trained, highly qualified teachers and coaches. Examine the opportunities your school offers students. Is there more that could be done to involve more students?

RESEARCH

Research supports that students who participate in extracurricular activities have higher academic achievement outcomes and a stronger sense of self-worth (Holloway, 2000). Students who are actively involved in school activities are less likely to drop out of school than their participating peers.

Stronger relationships among both peers and teachers that promote human development are developed as a result of student participation in extracurricular programs (Mahoney, 2000). According to McNeal (1997), the benefits of students being involved in extracurricular activities outweighs other factors that impact drop-out data such as race, socioeconomic status, and gender. A study by Holland and Andre (1987) concluded a direct correlation to participation in extracurricular activities in producing fewer negative behavior incidences and delinquency rates in schools.

INTERVENTIONS

Strong community partnerships can help in offering a wide array of after school activities. Local dance troops and art guilds can be a wonderful resource. Does your school tap into the expertise available in your local community? Clogging, other forms of dance, local musicians, story-tellers, woodworkers, gardening clubs, bird watching clubs, and chess and bridge clubs, to name just a few, are examples of missed opportunities in finding sponsors to head up a club-type activity.

Many businesses require employees and chief executive officers to be involved in community service. Give local leaders the opportunity to be a mentor to young people in becoming a sponsor of a school club or activity.

Take time during a faculty meeting to find out the talent that abounds in the community. Teachers are usually "in the know" and can quickly form a list. These local talents and volunteers, if approached with an opportunity to support the school, could expand the school's list of offerings.

REFERENCES

Holland, A., and Andre, T. (1987). Participation in extracurricular activities in secondary school: What is known, what needs to be known? *Sage Journals Review of Educational Research*, 57(4), 437–66.
Holloway, J. (2000). Extra curriculum activities: The path to academic success. *Educational Leaders*, 57(4).
Holloway, J. (2002). Extracurricular activities and student motivation. Retrieved from http://www.ascd.org/publications/educational-leadership/sept02/vol60/num01/-Extracurricular-Activities-and-Student-Motivation.aspx.

Mahoney, J. (2000) School extracurricular activity. *Child Development*, *71*(2), 502–6.
McNeal, R. B. (1997, March). High school dropouts: A closer examination of school effects [Electronic version]. *Social Science Quarterly*, *78*(1), 209–22.

11

"WITHIT" HIGH SCHOOL

There are more differences between schools than within a school. Schools and entire school districts vary from place to place. Particular schools in a district might be high performing, whereas others in the same district struggle to meet basic standards. Some schools that have a greater number of students with disabilities who face more barriers to learning outperform those with less. How do some schools get the job done when others remain persistently low performing? All schools have the opportunity to reach high levels of excellence, but many fall short.

Research reveals that few schools create systemic processes for implementing a set of transition plans (Mizelle and Irvin, 2000) to help students through these life-altering transition changes along their journey through the K-12 setting. Those schools that step to the plate oftentimes demonstrate a "withitness" where faculty, staff, and parents work systemically together to help all students succeed.

VIGNETTE

His name was Jeremy. His dad ran off and left Jeremy and his mom when he was five. Gramps died of lung cancer when he was seven. Mom worked three jobs to make ends meet while Jeremy helped care for his younger brothers and sisters, not to mention his grandma who is in a wheelchair and on disability.

Role models in his family were non-existent. Since his mom did not go to school past grade eight and his dad dropped out before graduating from high school, Jeremy was nervous about what to expect as he entered high school. He really wanted to be the first person in his family to graduate from high school, but he had doubts as to whether he has the wherewithal and the know-how to make it.

Jeremy does not know it yet, but he is one of the lucky ones. He will be attending "Withit" High School. His high school is keenly aware of the pitfalls and landmines that surround kids as they transition from middle school to high school. The school has developed a culture where faculty members are learners too.

Faculty members engage in studies and research topics before they implement any program or practice. In their quest to help students with a smooth transition from grade eight to grade nine, the teachers studied the literature that informs educators of this critical juncture in a student's life and how many students are lost in the transition when schools do not implement effective transition plans. The "Withit" High School faculty became knowledgeable about successful and proven transition plans before developing their own.

Early in his eighth-grade year, Jeremy noticed his classmates talking about "next year." If the truth be told, some of the fears and anxieties they shared were the same ones Jeremy felt but he was too macho to admit.

Jeremy's teachers seemed to have a plan to make the transition a smoother one. At the beginning of grade eight the middle school counselor held an assembly where Jeremy was introduced to the two high school counselors. Present in that same gathering were twenty high school upperclassman. His eighth-grade class was about two hundred students strong so dividing the twenty high school student mentors among the middle school students made a ratio of ten to one: ten students to one high school mentor.

Once assigned to the high school mentor, student groups quickly moved off to an area where they could more intimately talk with their mentor. Mentors gave out business cards that had their name, email, and phone number. On the card it had the list of activities the mentor was involved in, the mentor's hobbies, and their career interests. The mentors told the students to put the card in a safe place because next year, if they had any questions the school could not answer, the high school mentor was their personal "go to" person. The mentors told the eighth graders they would be meeting with them again the first week of school and throughout the coming year.

The mentors proceeded to tell the students what to expect academically, the supports services available, and response to intervention options. Jeremy had always thought these things were something designed for the "dumb kids." However, the "cool" high school mentor made it sound that you are smart if you seek help, admit what you do not know, and take advantage of help being offered at school. His mentor even admitted that he himself had taken advantage of these extra resources.

The mentor continued to talk about expected behavior at the high school, how to counter peer pressure, and how it was *not* cool to harass or bully others. His words matched a saying on his business card: "It's cool to learn and cool to care."

Jeremy had always heard about a resume that would someday be needed to land a job. The mentor shared an example of a resume outline and asked, "If *you* were applying for a job today, what would your resume look like?" He encouraged the students to start thinking *now* about what they would like to be when they grow up and to start setting goals.

He shared that employers will look at grades but they also want employees to be on time, not get in trouble, and show up ready to work. He also shared that being involved in school activities is important to employers. Being in various school activities helps you mingle with lots of different people and these experiences make you a better, more well-rounded person. He advised the students to become more aware of their grades, never be satisfied with grades below a C, and work toward being better than just average. He encouraged the students to set goals, to have no discipline infractions, to not miss school, and get involved in some type of school activity.

With regard to the resume, three references would be needed. The mentor told the students to build a positive relationship with at least three teachers who would agree to be a reference. Students could not just put three teachers' names down as a reference. Students had to go talk with the chosen teacher and get their permission to put their name on the resume. If a teacher did not feel comfortable being a reference, they were to tell the student why, what was needed to correct the situation, and to come back after improvements were made and see if the student earned the right to use them as a reference.

Later in the day, grade eight students found out the outline or resume building would become an activity in middle school advisory time. Each nine-week grading period students were charged to update the resume template provided. The resume let students see first-hand what they were doing—or not doing—in preparing for a career or job.

As the eighth-grade year progressed, "Withit" High School teachers worked collaboratively with the middle school in planning events to prepare students for the freshman year of high school. Teachers gave students a tour of the high school in the form of a scavenger hunt. Teachers arranged a teacher swap where high school freshman teachers came to the middle school and taught for a day. The school scheduled a session for middle school parents to meet with high school teachers and discuss high school expectations.

On four occasions, high school student mentors and high school teachers came to middle school events (band concerts, plays, sports, and dances). This provided opportunities for teachers to know the incoming students beyond the classroom. These transition activities made eighth graders see how much high school teachers genuinely cared about them.

By the time Jeremy got to the high school he had forged relationships with teachers and student role models. Jeremy may not have had the best roles models at home, but he felt a family of support at school as he looked forward to entering the high school. Because of these transition activities that the middle school and high school collaboratively developed, many of Jeremy's anxieties were relieved. He could now concentrate on doing the work at hand and focus on the task of learning rather than spending time concentrating on the little things that are really big things to kids in the transition. Jeremy believed the middle school and high school really understood kids.

Jeremy thought, *No wonder the school is often called "Withit" High School.*

RESEARCH

A study by Hertzog and Morgan (1999) informs educators that schools implement fewer than three transition activities. Studies reveal these same schools experience higher behavior incidences, a greater number of freshman failure rates, and an increase in dropouts. Most schools across the country do not work collaboratively between the middle school and high school to ensure a smooth transition into high school. Educators are forced to become reactive rather than proactive in addressing the needs of freshman students.

Grade nine is known as the "freshman bulge" because too many students fail to advance from grade nine to grade ten. That is due in large part as a result of the lack of a set of district-wide systemic plans in the transition from grade eight to grade nine. Freshman that cannot handle the rigors of the high school become lost in the transition.

To increase the chances of student success, middle and high school educators must work together to align curriculum, share individual student needs, communicate behavior expectations, and create a smooth transition (Williamson and Johnston, 1999). Knowing grade eight to grade nine is a critical time that can determine success or failure is important, but doing something about it is paramount. We must work together to stop the downward spiral by developing strategies that can counter the negative impact associated with the transition.

INTERVENTIONS

In these challenging economic times where money and financial resources are scarce, schools must look for innovative ways to work more efficiently and be more cost effective. Implementing transition activities cost nothing.

In the scenario with Jeremy, discuss the various transition activities "Withit" High School implemented. Can you see these being implemented in your school? Does the middle school and high school in your district have a working relationship to develop something similar?

Activities embedded in the "Withit" High School Transition Plan:

1. High school student mentors assigned to grade eight students.
2. Middle school/high school counselor assemblies/meetings.
3. Counselor meetings with students for dissemination of information on grades, behavior, support services.
4. A tour of the high school in the form of a scavenger hunt.
5. Parent information meetings for students transitioning to the high school.
6. Middle school advisory programs.
7. Teacher swap to build relationships before students enter the high school.
8. High school teachers attending middle school events to know students on a personal level: band concerts, dances, plays, sporting events, and so on.
9. Goal-setting activities that help students look to the future and develop an individual plan as they enter high school.

REFERENCES

Hertzog, C. J., and Morgan, P. L. (1998). Breaking the barriers between middle school and high school: Developing a transition team for student success. *NASSP Bulletin*, *82*(597), 94–98.

Mizelle, N., and Irvin, J. (2000). Transition from middle school into high school. *Middle School Journal*, *31*(5), 57–71.
Williamson, R., and Johnston, J. H. (1999). Challenging orthodoxy: An emerging agenda for middle level reform. *Middle School Journal*, *30*(4), 10–17.

12

QUESTIONS... QUESTIONS... QUESTIONS

Will I get lost? Can I keep up with classwork? Will I fit in? Who can I turn to if I have problems? How involved should my parents be as I enter high school?

These are just a few of the many questions middle school students ask as they enter high school. These questions left unanswered until the first week of a student's high school career can cause great amounts of fear and trepidation. If one starts anything off on the wrong foot it can result in students playing "catch up." And some students never *catch up.*

Just when a student needs to concentrate on more rigorous academics, these little things that so concern the adolescent student dominate student thinking. These little things truly are the big things, and educators need to validate what many students voice as issues of concern. Fears left unaddressed can start the downward spiral for many students that ultimately manifests itself into high absenteeism, an increase in tardiness, and an increase in failing grades that negatively impacts chances of high school success.

VIGNETTE

Terrell wondered what the high school was going to be like. His middle school had 580 students and fifteen students of that population were African American like him. Terrell worried if he would be made fun of, picked on, or accepted. He wondered about dating too. His mom and dad preferred he date an African American girl, but with the small minority population of students in his school, that was going to make dating a challenge.

Barb was a tiny thing at 4' 10". She was a strong student that felt she needed to have every book with her at all times. She had a locker assigned to her but she preferred to carry her books rather than take the time to fight the crowds in the hall and wiggle her way to her combination lock. Her backpack likely weighed as much as she did. Barb worried if she could get to class on time, if she would get lost, and how she would navigate the halls during class change. Being small in stature, she never saw anything at the middle school past people's armpits and elbows as she was bumped and jostled around during class change. She pictured high school upperclassman as giants!

Elmer just started to realize how poor his family was. In elementary school he was accepted alright and included in most everything the other kids in his class were doing. But in the middle school he began to see a division.

He heard about parties he was not invited to. He began to notice the brand names of clothes the "in crowd" wore. He began to hear snide remarks about off brand clothes, and he knew many of the off brand were the labels in what he wore. He feared the high school was going to be even worse.

If he was beginning to feel left out now, he wondered if he would be one of those kids eating at a lunch table all alone and the loner sitting along the wall at a school dance. He worried further about getting behind in his grades and being pulled out for remediation. He envied those kids whose parents went to college who had the know-how to help their kid at night with homework.

Tom, on other hand, was a perfectionist. Perhaps a better way to say it was his parents were perfectionists. Since elementary school his parents expected nothing but straight As from him. He felt he had to have the highest grade on state tests, a 4.0 average, and the highest ranking among his classmates. He surmised the high school would be even more rigorous. He worried whether he could maintain his streak of perfection. He began to obsess with this notion to be the best.

No one knew he was at the brink of a breakdown or that he had even contemplated suicide. He hoped there would be someone at the high school, some trusted adult, that he could confide in to help him get off this merry-go-round of perfectionism he was stuck on who could also reason with his parents.

Jenny was so creative. She did not dress like the other kids but that did not bother her at all. She felt there was some gift that she had been blessed with, and she was right. She could take a canvas and some charcoal pencils and draw the most beautiful pictures. Teachers recognized her efforts but classmates never did. She wondered why the football players and cheerleaders got all of the recognition and why other students did not see the beauty in the things she did. She always felt the schools she attended never showcased or promoted creativity and the arts. She could only hope that someday her gifts would be recognized and of some value.

Adults and educators many times forget what it was like to be an adolescent and emerging adult. Year after year, grade eight students leave the middle school and enter grade nine. These students may look like young adults in stature but they are nonetheless fragile young people full of all the fears and anxieties that come with developing into an adult. It is so critical that educators build meaningful relationships with students. Each and every student needs an adult mentor whom they trust and can confide in, someone who knows who they are, where they are from, and where they are going.

RESEARCH

The research of Hertzog and Morgan (1999) defines areas of concern to students and schools as they transition from one grade to another. Their research identified five categorical areas that schools can work collaboratively on in developing strategies that lessen the fears and anxieties students face as they leave the middle school and enter the oftentimes larger, more impersonal high schools.

The five categorical areas identified in this body of research include curriculum, safety and discipline, facilities, teachers/administrators and counselors, and general. Schools that pay special attention to these five areas and that develop transition activities to ease students into the high school can ensure a seamless and successful transition.

INTERVENTIONS

Discuss as a faculty the activities you have in place under the five categorical areas supported in the research. Share ideas of what could be done in the five areas.

Develop a budget of what it would take to implement these strategies. Develop a strategic plan that includes both the middle school and high school in the development of transition activities. Develop a timeline and activities for implementation.

Category 1: Curriculum

What could your school do to ease students and parents in the transition from the expectations of the middle school curriculum, expectations, rigor, grading scale, and so on?

Category 2: Safety and Discipline

What could your school do to ease the fears and anxieties of students as they enter the high school and the new behavior expectations? How do you inform students of the high school procedures for reporting harassment and bullying incidences?

Category 3: Facilities

What activities does your school have in place to familiarize incoming high school freshman with the new, often larger high school building?

Category 4: Teachers/Administrators and Counselors

What are things teachers could do to ensure a smoother transition to the high school for grade-eight students? Are there specific things teachers could do? Administrators? Counselors?

Category 5: General

What innovative things could your school create to help freshman with their entry into the high school? Summer transition camps? Freshman intervention clinics? Other?

REFERENCE

Hertzog, C. J., and Morgan, P. L. (1998). Breaking the barriers between middle school and high school: Developing a transition team for student success. *NASSP Bulletin.* 82.

Hertzog, C. J., and Morgan, P. L. (1999). Making the transition from middle level to high school. *High School Magazine*, 6(4), 26–30.

Mizelle, N., and Irvin, J. (2000). Transition from middle school into high school. *Middle School Journal*, 31.

ABOUT THE AUTHORS

Carol J. Christian, EdD, has served as teacher, coach, principal, and professor in Kentucky with over thirty years of experience. She has co-authored *Privileged Thinking in Today's Schools: The Implications of Social Justice and Heart to Heart*. She was selected to serve in Kentucky's Highly Skilled Educator Program working with low-performing schools. She holds degrees from Eastern Kentucky University and a Doctorate in Education from the University of Louisville.

C. Thomas Potter II, EdD, has served the education profession as a teacher, principal, and superintendent in Kentucky for over twenty-two years. He is one of twenty-five selected superintendents to serve in a leadership cohort sponsored by the National Institute of School Leaders. He holds a Master of Arts in Secondary Education and a doctorate in Educational Administration from Morehead State University.

Kevin S. Koett, EdD, has served as a mentor, instructor, and student affairs professional in higher education for over twenty-eight years. He has served in a variety of roles at six different institutions and has been recognized for his servant-leadership as the first recipient of the Joe Buck Service Award. He holds a Bachelor of Arts in

Social Studies Teaching from Augustana College (SD), a Master of Science in Higher Education Administration from Syracuse University, and a Doctorate in Educational Leadership from Morehead State University.

www.ingramcontent.com/pod-product-compliance
Lightning Source LLC
Chambersburg PA
CBHW032031230426
43671CB00005B/278